# OVER TO YOU
## An Exchange of Poems

**Stellasue Lee**
**David Widup**

**Bombshelter Press**
**Los Angeles, 1991**

Bombshelter Press, 6421½ Orange St., Los Angeles, CA 90048

**ISBN 0-941017-23-0**

PRINTED IN THE UNITED STATES OF AMERICA

Cover Art: Tact Communication Group, Graham Clark - President

Special thanks to Jack Grapes for his constant encouragement and boundless joy in celebrating life through art.

**BOMBSHELTER PRESS**
6421½ Orange St.
**Los Angeles, CA  90048**

**For Marie and Geoffrey**

# CONTENTS

Ben comes in while I'm working,
and says "Hi, Dad".
Not stopping, I ask him where he's been.
He says the beach.
I say nothing.
He walks away minutes later,
saying he's going to lay down for awhile.
I say nothing.
I think about being a bad parent a lot these days.

The road isn't alway well lit.
Now summer comes along,
steamy with heat,
and I thought I knew myself well
and just how I listened to my words,
every syllable, as if there might
be music between the lines.

I sleep naked these days,
nothing but skin and sheets,
even in the cold.
It's better for my health,
better for my marriage.
Twenty years is a long, long time.
I cannot let go.
Maybe if we had gone to Hawaii,
or kicked her Mom out,
or waited to have kids,
or stayed in Wyoming,
or cared about us more,
maybe it would have been easier.
It wasn't, but then again,
nothing comes easy anymore.
Nothing.

But I haven't said eveything.
After all, summer is three months long.
I sit in a room with diamond panes
reflecting all the colors of the rainbow.
I think I'm in touch with things,
then I see myself walking along the street
just past the window.
The steam rising from the sidewalk,
I wonder if there are two of me.
The one seen sitting inside this room,
and the one walking along outside.

# 1. The Kitchen dw

I stand at the entrance to the kitchen,
the cluttered counters brightly lit
by the harsh white fluorescent lights.
The place is a mess.
Dirty dishes by the sink and on the table.
A glass half filled with old milk on one counter,
another with Pepsi behind the sink.
The hand towel is on the floor in front of the stove.
The microwave door is open,
the hardened remains of an exploded burrito inside.
The sink is filled with dishes and discarded food.
The dishwasher is empty.
There is no milk in the refrigerator,
it smells like old food.
The garbage can is filled to the top,
and an almost empty TV Dinner tray
lays half spilled on the floor
leaning against the side of the can.

An ant is crawling across
the linoleum floor towards the sink.
On the panel above the stove,
a light green 3M Post It Note
with my warning from last week -
"no chores, no privileges!"

These brats will use me up and throw
my ragged ass on the garbage heap.
They suck the blood from my veins,
suck the water from my stomach
before it refills my polluted cells,
suck the puss from my hard heart,
they will suck me dry,
my skin will fall off,

my bones will brittle and crack and break,
my eyeballs will roll from their sockets
down my angry face and over the dirty kitchen floor
and run right over that fucking piss ant.

I scream and pound on the kitchen table,
Fuck em, the bastards!
Fuck their tired, lazy, unkept souls.
I hope the shitheads drown in their own garbage!
I hate this mess!

# 2. Standing Upright

The morturary left a note taped to the door,
announcing my Mother's death.
Trained, I supposed
in the delicate art of disclosure.
It was a card, like I use
to send recipes to friends.
On the day she died,
the same date my Father had died
three years earlier, I think,
gray rain...some master bright light plan
to crack me apart.  I stand land upright
but don't see any humor unfolding.

No strip mined, fly in the face set up,
no put-down event
is going to take me out.
Let this be understood;
I will survive.
They'll know it, whoever
they are
and I refused to see my Mother
like that in death.

I am twenty-six
and childless.  My own
mortality at stake.
No child comes forth.
No kin of mine.
No blood of my blood courses
through young, strong veins.
No child to suckle sweet
at my breast.

The dream continues
for twenty-four years.
Each new day I survive
mounds of blood clots,
endless rivers of red,
until it is clear,
even to me,
that one of us has to die.
The dream
or
me.
I think,
me
or
the dream?

I am six
and take care of my dolls.
They need to be dressed
and fed.
They need to be loved.
Mostly loved.
Grown-ups ask,
"What do you want to be
when you grow up?"
And I say,
"A mother,
with lots of children."

They wring their hands
at such single-mindlessness,
such tunnel vision.
I can tell you, not once, I swear,
not once, did I conceive of a life

without children.
Always, there was to be
one at the hem of my dress,
one at my breast.

Now that child's dream
is dead.
The mother and
the father dead.
And what of the dead?
They stare with sightless eyes.
Stone cold hands rest
over empty, beatless chest.
Hands that wring no more.

Let this be understood:
I continue.
Dreamless.
Bloodless.
Childless.
I stand,
knucklebones intact.

This was going to be so nice and civil;
I write a poem,
she reads it
and it sparks something in her.
Anything.
A phrase like
"splashes of midnight blue pigments
on a dead white wall"
or maybe it's the theme
like dead babies
or dead mothers
or mothers that are babies.
Then she writes from the spark,
feeds on the idea,
cuts it loose,
reaches through the nighttime sky
and grabs the tiny star
and brings it into her mouth.
And it would go on this way
back and forth.
Kind of like a friendly game
of lawn tennis
on a cool blue Sunday afternoon,
with iced tea and cookies afterward.

But no, oh no.
These are not little sparks
and neat, clean lines
filled with cute, curled words.
No.
These are kick in the gut,
slap in the face,
ice down the back of the pants,
hair grabbing poems.

These are "mounds of blood clots",
"suck the puss from my hard heart",
line after line.
This is championship tennis
on hard courts
in the hot noonday sun,
volley after volley;
game after game;
set after set;
match after match;
with grit in our teeth
and sweat poring out of us.
Hard serves hit chalk lines
faster and faster
as bones and muscles hurt,
cramp,
scream for rest
and calm, easy practices
followed by late afternoon iced tea and cookies.
These poems,
sent one after the other,
are not practice.
They are the real thing.
I want dark, wild passion,
and damn it all!
I get it
and a kick in the shins
and a small smile.
My serve,
over to you!

# 4. No Game sl

I've played tennis,
played seven maybe eight
hours a day. Sometimes twelve
on Sunday.
I know how the ball hits
soft on a lawn green court
in England.

I've come off a court in Spain
with red clay dust covering my
fair skin, turning my ash hair
strawberry blond.

I've played singles, doubles,
round robins. I've played
Wimbledon, bend-your-knees,
hit-the-ball-hard tennis.

I've socked-it-to-'em on the West Coast,
East Coast, Hawaii.
Tahiti, Fiji, Austria,
France, Belgium and all the places
in between.

Driving West on Roscoe Boulevard
a car runs the light,
broadsides me.  I am
pinned in the wreckage like
a butterfly under glass.

Doctors say I'll never walk again.
They shake their heads
and mumble something
that sounds like years of recovery.

I say, I'm going home...home to heal.

Then I play tennis all day,
practice my backhand,
forehand, overhead, smash.
I hit buckets of balls
and work through days of pain,
nights of agony on my game...my game.

Three months later
I'm back on the court
holding my old racket,
lacing up run-over shoes,
fastening my short, white skirt.
I run, bend my knees and
hit the ball...hard.

"$230 a month isn't much,
especially with a wife and a baby"
my Sergeant Major said,
his thin alcoholic face a mask,
deep lines carved into hard skin.
Only his eyes moved, and not much,
no telling what's inside.
His office smells like dust and envelopes.
I'm having trouble breathing,
my lungs are stiff and hurt,
my palms are cold and wet.
I leave without a word.

The others said much the same,
the message loud and clear -
I won't make it on the outside,
can't take it as a civilian.
I'll be broke, won't have money for college.
My baby will go hungry,
my wife will leave me.
I'll beg them, beg them
to let me back in, but they'll be full up.
I won't make it on my own.

And I let them make me scared,
forgetting that I lived on my own since I was 16,
graduated High School at 17,
was in Vietnam at 18,
was the youngest NCO in the Air Force,
was the youngest NCO in Vietnam,
survived Tet 1969 at Nuy Bah Dihn
on the north perimeter,
(nobody here gets out alive!),
stuck the muzzle of my .38 in Wild Bill's mouth

and pulled back the hammer at 19,
carried my girl, screaming, stark raving mad
from her house to the Police car,
butcher knife and all at 19,
buried my obedient guilt deep, deep down at 20.
I let them make me forget
that I knew how to make it.

And he was right,
$230 a month wasn't much money,
but my baby didn't starve,
and my wife didn't leave,
college paid me to stay
and I have never begged,
never,
anyone for anything,
let alone the right
to serve a dying life
in an ugly green uniform.

# **6.** The Gift

"Consider the lilies of the field,
how they grow; they toil not,
neither do they spin." Mat. 6:28

In the hills of Saint Ann, Jamaica,
I walk where walking unaccompanied
is not recommended.

Children run circles around me
keeping their distance.  Rag-a-muffin
souls, bone lean, crusted with
years of dirt.

One ventures near, hands
out-stretched. Says, "Miss,
do you have any money?"
I pull coins from my pocket
and give him all I have.
The children run back
into the countryside.

The next day I say I'm going shopping
but instead walk into the hills.
Eyes follow me. I hear
the scampering of feet over rocks.

A few yard off the path,
I take a hundred American
one dollar bills,
and toss them
into the wind.
It's only right, I think,
for this gift to be delivered
by the wind.

She sits in a small ball in the dark,
her sea green terrycloth robe
wrapped tightly around her, neck to ankle,
the sash tied in a double knot.
She is staring at the TV test pattern.
Her eyes do not move off the screen,
they do not move but to blink.
One arm rests firm against her stomach,
its open hand holding the other arm's elbow,
the forearm standing straight up,
at the end a lit cigarette
held still in space just next to
her small, grey lips.
She pulls on the filter
and the tip glows hot and long.
She sucks up over an inch of paper and tobacco
before she exhales out, slow and steady.

She once spent money like water,
after her husband died,
the one she left the sisterhood for,
the one she treated like Jesus Christ,
the one whose invalid feet
she washed with soapy water and acid tears,
the one, the only one, she ever loved.
She bought clothes and cars and a trip to Hawaii
with the insurance money,
and acted like someone who
had a right to be happy.
She spent money like she mattered
and it didn't.

Before it all ran out,
she went really crazy

and gave it all away.
She gave cash to strangers on the street,
wrote checks, big checks that didn't bounce,
to the Church she left
and could never go back to.
She gave it as loans
to brothers and sisters.
that were never repaid.

She gave it all away.
She kept none of it for herself.
Not one penny left.
The checking account was empty,
there was no stash in her mattress,
the stocks and bonds
in the safety deposit box were missing,
silver dinnerware and jewelry vanished,
there was nothing left
that anyone else would want.
She didn't have to pretend
she deserved it any longer.
It was all gone.

Just as the cigarette ash gets too long to stay,
she reaches over and puts the butt down
and walks to her small, open bedroom.
She lays on top of the mattress
in her robe and slippers
and stares at the ceiling,
her dark, wet eyes only move to blink
as she spends another night.

sl

Take the child
that just wants to know
how things work,
like a leg moving
in a hip socket
or what makes the ocean
water stay in one place
instead of just running
flat
over all the land.

Now, this child
grows up, lives a
crazy life, grows old.
Maybe grows mean,
like old Mrs. Harrington
up the street, and
one day the neighbors
realize nobody
has seen this person
in quite a while.
They stand around
in front of the house
and wonder what to do.

Meanwhile, days earlier,
she just laid down on
the front room sofa,
covered herself up
with a blue and white
checkered Afghan,
and drifted off
wondering if there really was

such a thing as Saint Peter
waiting at the pearly gates
and if angels had wings,
when a white light
appears at the end of a tunnel.

Moving in that direction,
she remembered reading
about reincarnation and
wondered again, if in fact,
this might all be true.

# 9. End of the Tunnel dw

Mom died alone,
in a small double bed
on a humid, July hot
New Jersey afternoon.
I know.  I wasn't there.

When she died,
she never saw a light
at the end of the tunnel,
wasn't drawn to some warm
guiding home place.

Make no bones about it -
she died the way she lived,
hard, drunk and crying.
And when she went, she was gone,
there was no in between.

Weeks before, on the phone,
after I ran away from her dying,
standing in a stranger's basement,
she said, "Come home.
You know how I can be."
I said I'd consider it and didn't.

Lying dead, stiff in bed,
her unkept grey black hair
spills across the white pillow,
her lips form a thin smile
because she sees
no light at the end of the tunnel.

When at last they told me
my husband was dead,
the whole hospital seemed
relieved.  The nurse
taking temperatures
looked directly at me.
The doctor put his arm
around my shoulder,
patted my hand,
and mumbled something
sounding like an outline
for a short story.
Young...Marry again...
Another child.
As if at that moment
I could think about
getting out of bed or
feeding the dog.

Here it is.
A twenty year old wife,
gives birth to a stillborn
child, and becomes a widow
all in one day.
Everybody jumps right in
pointing out how young she is,
and how she has her whole life
ahead of her.
Her husband and baby
aren't even buried yet.

They were right, in a way.
Thirty years later
I don't think about it much

but I didn't marry again
for another eighteen years
and there never was
another baby.

Things have always been too easy
for my oldest son, my oldest child.
It was too easy to get good grades,
so he didn't after a while.
It was too easy to hit home runs,
so he quit playing baseball at 15.
It was too easy to pretend to be free,
so he stayed at home.

And it was too easy,
that hot Saturday afternoon,
easy to get rid of the pain
by taking 35 Extra Strength Tylenol,
going upstairs into his bedroom,
locking the door, putting some music on,
laying down
and going to sleep,
to sleep,
sleep.

During our night together
in the Emergency Room
at our neighborhood hospital
the nurse made him drink
activated charcoal
and he puked black slime
for hours and hours.
It was on his face,
all over the sheets,
on the floor around the bed.
And then he puked nothing but air.
He was pale, sheet white,
with an IV tube stuck in his arm
and dark black circles under his eyes.

Black circles, his blood
on the white linoleum floor,
freshly waxed and buffed.
Black circles, red blood,
white floors, going to sleep,
to sleep, to sleep,
sleep.

He says
he didn't mean to kill himself,
he just wanted to make a statement,
you know, fight with a girlfriend,
things not going his way,
life isn't easy anymore,
college real tough,
wrecked the car a few weeks ago,
you know, make a statement,
go to sleep, go to sleep,
to sleep,
to sleep,
sleep.

It's eighty-five and the sun
weighs heavy on the back of my head.
The house is locked up
tighter than a drum
and I haven't any keys.

I go from window to door
to window, pushing,
praying for something to give.
Nothing had changed.
I stare in at the bed my step-daughter
sleeps in...the same one
she thinks about killing herself in
she says. I think,
it looks friendly enough.

The next window looks in on
the two easy chairs in my office.
They look back at me, fondly,
I'd like to think.
Around back I push the patio table under
the kitchen window.  It's locked,
of course.  But I stand on the table,
precariously balanced,
and look inside. Then imagine
myself fixing ice tea and
looking out to the gardens...
the sea.

"Get hold of yourself." I say,
as my knees crumple on to
the table top.  I spread across
the circumference like
spilt milk, sobbing out the years

of just scraping by and sacrifice,
all for an ungrateful kid who's
only thoughts are ending it all.
And I might have slept like that
in the shade, dreaming about
children and trouble.  Dancers,
these two.

After I think things over,
it seems perfectly clear.
I climb down from the table
and get a patio chair; lift
the chair high over my head.
With a force I didn't know possible,
I smash the window,
and giving no thought
to  broken glass,
head straight for the shower.

1323 Francine Ave. is a small ranch house
in a lower middle class subdivision
of Joliet, Illinois.
It's brick facade has been painted again and again.
It used to be white; it's blue now.
The house is filled with holes.
I know. I put most of them there
and tried to fill all the rest.

In blind, white hot adolescent rage I kicked,
punched and threw things around the house.
Life had done me wrong and I cried and screamed.
But mostly, I punched holes with my tight fist
in the unfinished plasterboard walls of the garage
that we used as a storage shed to hold the stuff
that wouldn't fit in the house.
It was filled with holes I put there
because my mother drank a bottle of Sherry before lunch
and then washed it down
with a quart of bourbon before dinner,
because my father was never around except to yell,
because we moved all the time and I had no friends,
because I was fat and ugly and stupid,
because I couldn't understand the teachers in school.
I punched a hole the day my older sister left
to go to college in Indiana.
That night I slept alone in the living room
on the sofa in my jeans with no blanket
and smoked a pack of Winstons before 4 AM.

And the hole I punched when Kennedy was shot
is just as big as the one from when
Susan Thomas' sister called to tell me
that Susan just wanted to be friends with me.

Once I hit a wall and behind was a stud beam.
It broke my hand in seven places.
It was months before I put another hole in the house.

But mostly, I tried to fill holes,
like the hole in my parent's marriage,
big enough to hold the Pacific Ocean,
and all their tears.
I tried to fill the bottomless hole in my mother's soul
with something besides booze
and the hole in my baby brother's life
with fun and games,
baseball in the back yard
and hockey on the ice covered street in winter
and sock football in the hallway when they were gone,
me on my knees and Rick on his feet.
Once, we knocked over the Hong Kong table
and bent the lip of the lower bronze disk.
We filled some holes that night.

But most of the holes wouldn't stay filled,
I kept putting me into the holes and they emptied
almost faster than I could pour me in,
and when that got to me,
I stopped filling and started punching.
Just before we moved, I had to fill
all the holes in the garage.
I admired them,
all 20 or 30 black spots of emptiness,
for over an hour before I went to work.
And I can't remember
filling even one
of those damn holes.

# 14. One Word

The wind was blowing up a gale
and I remember it had rained
all night but the occasion
eludes me just now.

It might have been anything.
A holiday, my graduation,
somebody's wedding.  It was
so long ago.

On paper
our skins turned
sepia.  Mother stands pretty,
as any cherished wife.

Dad walks in
from his other life
just long enough to take his
rightful place.

Brother is smiling from ear to ear
but I remember, Mom just cuffed
one of his ears, and now that I look
closer, I see it's not a smile

but rather a grimace
falling onto the rigid shoulders
of a small boy with a crew cut.
I stand apart, leaving a hole

between them and me, a hole
big enough to pass a bicycle through.
Wishing the hole still larger
like the distance of a continent maybe.

And if I know anything, there was
emptiness, too spent
even for anger, yet
I am smiling too.  I might
have survived that day better

if there had been a word
to sum it all up.
One word...to stuff in all the holes
our lives were making, but the right word

didn't come along for years
and then it took me longer still
to make it fit...dysfunctional.
We were a dysfunctional family.

Old pictures, baby pictures,
draw me in like gravity.
I stare at the montage for
hours, day after day.
Getting dressed after my shower
in the morning, I stare at it
by my desk and I'm late to work.
At night, getting undressed
in the too late, dim light,
I bend and stare at first one,
then another and another picture,
and it's 1 AM when I get to bed.

The kid is smiling,
big, honest, full teeth, eyes squinting,
smiling in almost every picture.
Here, in England walking out front
of the small house in coveralls and brown shoes,
smiling like he's stepping out on the town.
And in this one, two years old
and on the toilet, for God's sake,
grinning to beat the band.
Years later, at twelve, on the sofa
in his Uncle's house with brother and sister,
all of them smiling and happy.
No telling Mom and Uncle Bob
would both die in the next two years.

There's one with him
walking away from Mom,
her arm stretched out after him,
Sis looking up and asking God
about him like all older sisters do,
and he's got the biggest,

shit eating grin on his face........

The one I always end up on,
that makes me late to work
and lose so much sleep,
is with me and Mom at the beach.
I'm happy playing in the sand
and she is standing next to me smiling,
like she's got something to be happy about.
It's sunny and warm,
the sea is dark blue,
and I'm looking at the camera,
but she's just smiling at me.

In the later pictures,
the smiles go away.
There's one of the same three kids,
when they were all grown up.
The other two have thin smiles,
but I glare at the corner of the room.

Two boys came through my house
yesterday.  Two, wild with life
buddies, curving young bodies
into the furniture
only to wrestle free an instant
later. Handling things they had
never seen before with their
many fingers.

They went about whispering
and prodding each other.
Happiest when they could move
through the passage way
to all outdoors. Writing
arguments with pure energy.

Two small boys, sharing their
years and size but from different
seeds of restlessness. Each with
the beginnings of full grown men.
Speaking in code that only they
understand.  And then,
not all the time.

Something moved through me
at seeing them go,
slicing my heart open.
It wasn't about their going,
it was something about the way
their heads bent,
busy with seat belts.
And the way their arms raised
simultaneously, to wave.
I think it was the grin they both wore,

so pleased about things.

A siren went by
just at the precise moment
they disappeared from view.
The piercing sound warbling
in my heart, now half a century old.

Looking in my own rear view mirror,
I see my boy in the back,
sitting in his car seat,
seat belts strapped across his chest in an X.
He waves his chubby arms
at the cars as they pass by,
each one on both sides,
he doesn't care if they wave back.

When there are no cars,
he examines his fingers
with dark brown, round eyes
like a scientist bent over a microscope.
He moves them, twists them, tastes them.
He puts them in his ears and his eyes.

In an earlier rear view mirror,
the VW van we drove
from Wyoming to supposedly home,
I see him on the floor in his bassinet,
his head shoved into the corner,
sleeping all day long,
the headwinds howling so bad
it took days to get across Nebraska,
the sound of "$230 a month isn't much money"
ringing in my ears,
he sleeps on the floor of the van,
the rear view mirror aimed straight at him.

A year later in the same van,
he's in his car high chair
in the passenger seat next to Marie.
It's a sunny, warm Saturday morning in May
on the way to Mom Mom's house.

The VW van is not the first,
not the second,
but the third car
into the intersection
when it is rocked, hit hard, totaled
by a drunk 77 year old man.
Marie's seat belt holds her back
from the glass and big, round steering wheel,
but it cuts into her hip
all the way to the bone.
The kid, though, he goes flying right out the window
and onto the pavement
in the middle of Kirkwood Highway
and Newport Gap Pike,
only to be retrieved by a nurse
moments later without even a scratch.
I get to Mom Mom's hours later.
He's in his Mother's aching lap
playing with his fingers,
waving his chubby arms.

Where this drifted in from
I've no idea.
But the thought started right
after I washed a silk blouse,
took it outside dripping
with water, to dry
in the morning breeze.

About this half slip,
lace flowing from the hips
down, pure white, Glen Davis IV
gave me when I was just sixteen.

It came in a plain box
with a dozen layers
of white tissue paper.
And the softness of that tissue
at my finger tips, the
rustling noise when
I peeled the layers
back to reveal
this exquisite lace thing.

The week after, Glen parked
the car up on Mulholland
and asked me straight out
when my last period was.
Without even
giving it much thought,
I told him fourteen days ago.

Now thirty-five years later
this silk blouse hangs
waving in the wind

and droplets of water fall cold
over my face.
I watch the silk dry and remember
that white lace thing,
buried still, under other lace things
not nearly as delicious.

I swear, I don't think
I had any hormones back then.
But they did come,
later.

Lace covers things I want,
places that tease,
parts just slightly too secret.

White lace slips hang loose
from sharp hips
and the aching pelvis underneath
forms two thin crescents of desire
faintly outlined against white lace.

Black lace covers long legs
with curve below curve,
the lace bunches at the bend
behind the knee that asks
in a husky whisper
for me to run my fingers
through the thin crease,
gently separating lace from lace.

Red lace, intricate with mosaic patterns,
covers young breasts,
small, hard nipples
almost pushing through
beg for my tongue
to run the course,
find the opening in the maze
and hold its hard, dark
essence in the hot, quick moisture of me.

Lace covers delicate, special places,
cherished regions,
Lace covers and conceals.

My right elbow hurts.
Last week, it was my left thumb
or was it my knee?
It hasn't always been like this.
Just a short time ago
I leapt from the morning bed,
made it quick
to seal in the warmth.
Ran, mostly naked,
in some lace thing
just long enough
to cover the bare.
I didn't even own a robe.

Back then, diamond stars
ran up the heels of my shoes.
Now, it's this elbow,
my thumb, these knees.
They sing their own odd songs.

Passing by a store window,
I see this wonderful lace slip
the color of Champagne.
Exquisite French lace.
It cost a fortune
but I buy it anyway,
bring it home and wear it
to bed when the night comes.

There is a sound lace makes
moving through the air,
cooling in flight, lingering
a little, before it comes to rest
on the bedroom floor.

Hearing that sound
brought everything back to me.
All of it,
the leaping,
feeling that young,
that pretty,
that loved.

I'm thinking about being alone,
leaning against the porch rail.
It's cold here in the mountains,
even in mid May.
I stare past the tree tops
into the high desert air,
the rail at my belt pressing into me,
I barely notice it.

There's a scrub brush covered mesa
standing alone, just up the hill
from the hot dusty floor below.
I'm thinking about being alone
and staring across forever scenes -
the Grand Canyon
in December cool dry whiteness,
the Pacific Ocean due west of Santa Maria
beating the rough sand over and over,
here on top of the mountains
that stand above the killing desert -
all these looks into alone
hold me captivated in a trance,
I cannot stop looking, taking it all in,
I'm stuck like a hard anchored boat.
Beautiful alone
is the best of all worlds.
Right now, I need nothing else.

But, beautiful alone
isn't good enough
day to day
when kids need money,
a ride to the softball game,
another answer,

when they need to scream the anger of childhood pain
against my granite parent facade,
when my work demands
more knowledge than I have,
more time than the clock has,
more effort than I have energy,
more caring than I have commitment,
more denial than my mask can hide.

Then, during the long, long hours
of my everyday life,
then the past beautiful alone
is not nearly enough
and I need someone
to make beautiful.

Where could I have been these hours
to wake like this, drained of all
resources, spent in the darkness
that invades light
and sends the sun boiling
into the Western sea.
It brings a dank so profound,
just when I've given up all hope,
this crescent shaped silver light
hangs from mid air
hinting of a brighter tomorrow.
I'm saying, this night has robbed me
of any rest.  When the light finally
does make an appearance
I am forced to think of my daily ways.

I make my way, racing through debris towns,
towns littered with lives.  I think,
"There are men everywhere."
I look for the poet male
whose aged, crusted life
has not left him lame.
Early on, I was caught by tragedy,
held fast in the name of love.
Rigidly, this left me grown up
with miles of useless information
by examples.
Now this.
Tethered,
going down for the count,
in darkness,
swaying, and for what?
No one cries when I leave the room.

Picking my way along slippery rocks
at the bottom of a canyon,
I see sky overhead.
The clouds move peacefully,
seemingly at one with the earth.
This is no comfort.

All people should be born blind.
Then touch, that communication,
would unlock doors
to every heartfelt condition.
This world could survive through
eyelids closed and fingers that see no better.
Lying in the arms of a man,
touching places to please him,
touching places no one has touched,
a hard heart, touching the needy places,
the places that feed a soul,
touching blind, touching beauty
through closed eyes,
touching and being touched.

I am absent, yes, formless,
These cinders in life smart,
just cries on a muffled city.
Guileless, it's late.
A portrait of light...crumbles.
We are at the end of a century.
My years give me little hope for a future.
I no longer sleep
through the night and time alone
grows longer.
Day, oh day, it's a good thing
the mirror is covered in dust.

# 23. Not Just Day and Night   dw

Here, on the edge of the Pacific,
it's not just day and night.
After night but before daylight
is thick cloudy dawn.
There's light to see,
but the bright sun is not yet here
to put life under the harsh spotlight.

Everyone is alone in thick cloudy dawn,
alone in their thoughts of work and play.
Traffic moves in slow motion,
the wind is soft and steady,
it's neither hot or cold,
the rails sing soft with freight trains rolling,
coffee tastes as sweet as aged wine,
I make music in my head,
time stands almost still.
Nobody sees us leave the room.
The house is dark and quiet.

I'm reading the paper,
pretending to care about events I don't understand.
I'm drawn away from the news
to the ads for things I can't afford to buy.
It's easier for me to be interested
in what I want rather than what I do not know.
My coffee cup empty,
I walk to the counter and fill it.
I hear my clock radio go off upstairs,
the dogs jump to the floor and scratch
as Marie rolls over and lays on her back.
One of the kids turns on the shower.
I walk back to the kitchen table
and sit down as the sun burns through the clouds.

Another part of the day begins.
If I could choose to live my life,
I'd live a month or two straight
in early morning dawn,
thick clouds deadening the noise of life,
like a layer of blankets on an unmade bed.
I would do the things I never do,
like stare at a bird until I saw it good,
or read the news and not the ads,
or write a poem from beginning to end,
or stay awake all night,
or sleep all day,
or walk for miles and miles
along the quiet city streets
softened by the dull light through thick clouds.

I am not afraid of night's blackness
or daytime's harsh light.
I am just tired of wrestling with my sanity in the dark
and being only for others in the day.
Thank God,
it is not just day and night.

# 24. On the Sound

Here on the Sound,
the Strait, they call it,
the whitecaps toss about.
It's rough, and
a couple of small boats
are still out there
making a run for safety.

Earlier today I took a walk
in the woods.  The wind,
high in the evergreens,
ruffled me up pretty good.
I could have been
the last person on earth.
My God, I was lonely.
I walked to the graveyard
for some comfort.
Then kept right on walking
into town.
I rubbed elbows with strangers,
sipped a cup of brew
at the Coffee House then
bought a huge bouquet of flowers.

I walked so far
the flowers were half dead
by the time I got them in water;
the wind dogging my every step.

I think it might rain tonight.
One of these storms
without thunder would be nice.
I'm not going to
let the fire die tonight.

I'll keep all the lights burning.
Then I'll converse
with rattling windows
through the long darkness
and wait until love returns.

Fires rage through me
day after day,
night after night.

Bourbon straight
burns my throat on the way
to killing the pain
that roars through my veins
like thunderclap hard lightening.
The sunlight on my face feels like ice.

Fires in my brain
consume my thoughts
and generate acrid anger,
the smoke of fires too hot,
eating up wet, young foliage
in my head.

A poker hot, rose glow
burns in my chest
all the time.
It's always there,
throwing off heat from a heart
never held in grace
by a soft loving hand
for no other reason
than it is here
and it is mine
and it is needy.

Fire, roar hot,
range wild over dry, tinder land
and throw excess high
as black sooty smoke

that chokes all who dare to pass by.
Fires, roar on!
You consume me whole
and I walk on ...........hot,
waiting and burning.

We sit cradling cups of hot coffee,
needing the warmth, but neither of us
really liking the dark substances
with its thin layer of grease
floating over the top.  We both
pour milk into the cup, changing
the color, hiding the film.

It never makes things right
or softens the words spoken harshly.
Words, sparked with accusations,
lighting bonfires of rage.

After the flames die down,
after our hearts cool hard again,
he turns from me and looks
out the window, perspiration
still glistening on his face.

I am cold. Cold with the fear
at never feeling safe.
Is it possible, I wonder,
love somehow diminishes
each of us?

I didn't get to go to summer camp
when I was a kid.
There was never enough money.
So I've signed up for a writers' conference,
ten days on the Sound.
I'm going to walk in the woods,
flake out on the beach,
attend class and
go out dancing every night.
Hey, I'm going to feel like a
kid again, only this time
I've got money and I can
spend it just the way I want.

Now that I'm getting on in my life,
the sun shines brighter and the trees are greener.
Nothing is too simple for me today.
I never tire of looking at waves hit the beach,
dragging the rough sand back to sea
and hitting the shoreline again.
I still pinch myself to see if the things I have now are real.
Yesterday, I said goodbye to someone I love
and there wasn't even one tear in my eye.
I've found my work, I don't feel lost.
I don't need to look different than I am anymore.
I'm learning to like the clutter in the house.

I'm not sure why it took so long
to give myself permission to have fun.
I don't remember any of the school books
saying that life was so demeaning
having fun was a sin.
I intend to make up for lost time.

The man and woman at the next booth
are fighting over the check.
He loses, she pays.
He doesn't know how to be a man,
pay with confidence or pass and smile.
I didn't know how to be a man,
how to hold my baby girl in my arms
when she was sick and alone
and not be angry at her for screaming,
how to stroke my wife's back,
how to live in poverty with grace,
knowing that what I loved to do
was the only right thing to do -
teach, write, love, learn.
I learned to be a man too late for my kids,
and, maybe, for my wife.
But I learned in time for me,
just barely.